The Lost Lunchbox

by Cara Torrance

illustrated by Berta Maluenda

OXFORD

UNIVERSITY PRESS

AUSTRALIA & NEW ZEALAND

Chimpanzee had lost her pink lunchbox.

She was so sad.

Is that it?

"Can you help me out, Bat?" Chimpanzee said. "I have lost my lunchbox."

"It's not up in the tree," said Bat. "That is just my bright pink coat."

Chimpanzee kept looking for her lunchbox.

"No, it's just my hat," said Snail.

Chimpanzee went on looking.

"My lunchbox is in the pond," she said.

"It's not with me," said Fish.

"Now I can see it!" said Chimpanzee. "It's my lunchbox."

It was not her lunchbox.

"That is just my socks," said Baboon.

They were bright pink, too.

"My lunchbox is lost," said
Chimpanzee with a gulp.

"That is pink, but it's not my lunchbox," said Chimpanzee.

Chimpanzee pointed, "I see it!"

Chimp had her lunchbox.

"You are a champ, Chimp!"
said Chimpanzee.